Soul Survivor

*reflections & life lessons for parents
from an abandoned child*

Lon W. Flippo

Copyright © 2010 by Lon Flippo

Cover design by Dawn M. Brandon

All rights reserved.

No part of this book may be reproduced in any form or by any electronic or mechanical means including information storage and retrieval systems, without permission in writing from the author. The only exception is by a reviewer, who may quote short excerpts in a review.

Printed in the United States of America

First Printing: October 2010

ISBN 978-0-9840680-5-0

Scripture quotations marked KJV are taken from The Holy Bible, King James Version. Scripture quotations marked MSG are taken from THE MESSAGE. Copyright © 1993, 1994, 1995, 1996, 2000, 2001, 2002. Used by permission of NavPress Publishing Group. Scripture quotations marked NIV are taken from the HOLY BIBLE, NEW INTERNATIONAL VERSION®. Copyright © 1973, 1978, 1984 by International Bible Society. Used by permission of Zondervan Publishing House. All rights reserved.

*To Uncle Ed and Aunt Winnie Spigle.
You saved my life.*

*And to all those who have invested a lifetime to
raising abandoned children.*

Contents

Acknowledgments ix

Introduction 1

Reflections 5
    Innocent 9
    Abandoned 13
    Alienated 21
    Secure 27
    Lonely 31
    Frightened 37
    Determined 41
    Angry 47
    Guilty 51
    Tempted 59
    Released 63
    Hopeful 67

Life Lessons for Parents 71

- Children Need a Place to Call Home 75
- Children Need Responsibilities 79
- Kids Need Friends Who Are Headed in the Right Direction 83
- Parents Need to Come to Terms with Their Past 85
- Build Character through Discipline 89
- Show Children Where to Find Wisdom beyond Their Years 93
- Be a Dream Builder, Not a Dream Killer 95
- Give Kids Less Showtime and More Playtime 97
- Conclusion 99

Acknowledgments

Special thanks to Family Community Church and senior pastor Bill Buchholz. You gave me the opportunity to grow and expand my learning and life-cycle. I will always be grateful.

Dr. Wayde Goodall, advisor and friend. Thank you, Dr. Wayde, for your support and encouragement. You are a giant for leaders.

David Tieche, youth pastor, Family Community Church—a gentleman and a scholar. Your creative skills are awesome!

My children, Ashley and Wesley. You have been my front-and-center-of-life stage. I love you and believe in you, always.

My amazing wife, Chris. You are the greatest gift in my life. None of this is, will, or can be possible without you. I Love you tons!

Introduction

> A child is a person who is going to carry on what you have started.... He will assume control of your cities, states, and nations. He is going to move in and take over your churches, schools, universities, and corporations. The fate of humanity is in his hands.
>
> ABRAHAM LINCOLN

I've invested my life in people—helping them make better decisions, teaching children to make wise choices, coaching parents on spiritual training—and believing that every child has potential to soar and become something great. But sometimes I wonder. I doubt.

Am I making a difference, or is a child's future determined by fate? If circumstances cause lasting pain and alter a child's path, will the soul survive? Can the psyche thrive? Does the spirit hope? Having grown up in the midst of the storm of abuse and the silence of abandonment, can a child grow into a relatively healthy father or mother? Will she have an impact on the world? Will he become a contributing member of society? Or is survival—mere existence, struggling to endure—a child's only hope?

Can the abandoned children, those with gaping wounds in their souls, grow up and live fruitful, productive lives? Why do some appear destined to repeat the sins of the fathers, to continue the cycle of abuse and poverty, perhaps becoming addicts, dropouts, and delinquents? Certainly the scientific data suggests that circumstances and DNA are more powerful than the will of man and God.

But what about those who don't follow in the fateful footsteps of their forefathers? In an ideal world, where selfish ambition is absent, children would be born to parents who truly love and protect them. In a perfect world, parents would all love, protect, and provide for their children. But this is not an ideal world. Not all children are born into loving homes. Some are physically abused. Others are neglected, ignored, and left to fend for themselves; or they are emotionally abused, called names, ridiculed, and demeaned by their own parents. These children's bodies may remain intact, but their spirits and confidence wither. Some even die at the hands of their mom or dad.

A growing number of children face emotional neglect. Parents may feed and clothe their children, take them to day care and pick them up, and claim to love their children without ever nurturing their souls and spirits. They may even overindulge them—with technology, clothes, and toys. Such children grow up valuing things above people and relationships. They repeat the cycle, passing along the same attitude to their own children—unless good people with good intentions intervene.

Abuse comes in many forms, but most abused children don't shrivel up and die. They don't become serial killers or mobsters. Most grow up to be relatively normal people who often are better parents than their own.

What makes the difference? Forty-five years removed from my biological parents' destructive influences and behaviors, I wonder: why did I survive when others didn't?

One college professor told me I was a statistical anomaly. As a close friend of the people who raised me, he had firsthand knowledge of my history. When I consider my own story, I doubt God less. I believe more. I continue teaching for life-change.

Sometimes the difference parents and teachers make isn't visible for years. It's one lesson, one day, and one child at a time. Sometimes the investment is in the life of our own child. Sometimes it's through the influence we have on a friend's child, a student, or a nephew. We must seek to be difference makers. The fate of humanity depends on it.

PART 1

Reflections

Invictus

Out of the night that covers me,
Black as the Pit from pole to pole,
I thank whatever gods may be
For my unconquerable soul.

In the fell clutch of circumstance
I have not winced nor cried aloud.
Under the bludgeonings of chance
My head is bloody, but unbowed.

Beyond this place of wrath and tears
Looms but the Horror of the shade,
And yet the menace of the years
Finds, and shall find, me unafraid.

It matters not how strait the gate,
How charged with punishments the scroll,
I am the master of my fate:
I am the captain of my soul.

WILLIAM ERNEST HENLEY
BOOK OF VERSES, 1888

1

Innocent

> He drew me up from the desolate pit.
> PSALM 40:2 RSV

The man paged through the piles of papers and photos. It was hard to believe that nearly fifty years of his life could be reduced to a few shabby boxes of certificates, ribbons, trophies, and photographs, static images of events that evoked no memories. He was preparing to move his family. He had a new position in a new town. Was it possible to discard even more mementos of his small existence? He reluctantly shuffled through some old love letters and cards from his wife and children.

From the corner of his eye, he glimpsed a picture peeking from beneath the pile. He carefully pulled aside the paper and picked up the photo. Little Betsy, his only sibling, and a redheaded, freckle-faced boy—a younger version of himself—smiled back. How he loved and cared for his younger sister. Even though they fought like cats and dogs as teenagers, he was there for her when it mattered. He could not remember when or where the photo had been taken.

Memories cascaded through his mind like water flowing swiftly over a rocky creek. His mind meandered to a time and place in the distant past...to stories aunts and uncles had repeated about his parents and early childhood—then suddenly he found himself retreating into his childhood fantasy of what should have been.

Peoria, Illinois, 1959
The blond, blue-eyed, twenty-year-old man jumped in his Chevy Impala and roared away from Harrison, Arkansas, heading to a new life in Peoria, Illinois. He had his first real job—with Caterpillar, one of the largest manufacturers of equipment for moving dirt, rock, and other heavy items for construction. There he met a woman. They had a wildly happy time. They laughed. They played. They fell in love. They made love. She became pregnant. They married.

Peoria, Illinois, 1960
It's a boy! A boy. The father was speechless. His firstborn, a son, was...beautiful. Baby's brown eyes squinted at the light. His hair stood on end, orange as a carrot. The adoring father counted the fingers—one, two, three, four, five. He looked at the

other hand: one, two, three, four, five. Toes all there. The tiny face was lit up like a Christmas tree, radiant and pink.

The father left the hospital and called his eldest brother, James. Money was tight, but it was worth the expense of a long-distance phone call to share the news. Then he returned to the hospital to see his young wife, Judy. She looked tired, but she glowed as she held their newborn son.

"We'll call him Lon William, honey. That's a wonderful name. Isn't he something? Look at his tiny fingers." She kissed them and looked at her husband, the corners of her mouth gently curling upward. Her eyes filled with tears of love and joy.

The child's early years were filled with peace and harmony. When he was hungry, his mother fed him. When he was uncomfortable, she changed his diaper and held him to her bosom. Two years later, a little sister, Elizabeth, joined the happy family.

The children grew strong and beautiful. Lonnie's delightfully carrot-colored hair shimmered in the sunlight. With his round, freckled face and sparkling brown eyes, people said he should have been on television. He was energetic and full of life. Beth was petite and quiet. She rarely talked. But she could run. Even the boys couldn't keep up with her, in spite of her short legs. Lonnie and Beth believed that their mother loved them—that she didn't want to leave.

But then he reminded himself, as he looked at the photos, that this was wishful childhood fantasy, much like an imaginary friend. He thought, I still can't remember anything prior to my fifth year. Yet, after all these years and life experiences, my mind is still drawn back to the fantasy. Why does it still sting to remember the past? It was so long ago yet still so stirring to the mind and spirit.

2

Abandoned

> Before I shaped you in the womb, I knew all about you.
> Before you saw the light of day, I had holy plans for you.
> JEREMIAH 1:5 MSG

Harrison, Arkansas, 1964

The small, white house stood at the top of the hill. Like a lighthouse on a wave-worn coast, it rose from the ground as a father, two uncles, and two children drove up the dusty dirt road. It looked peaceful and serene as the long, dry, lonely trip to the back hills of Arkansas came to a close. Little did anyone know how, for two innocent children asleep on the floorboards of the Chevy pickup, the world would change forever behind the walls and doors of that little house.

Within days the boy could not recall what his mother looked like. What color was her hair, her eyes? What was the shape of her face or the contour of her frame? As he grew older, he overheard stories of those early years, stories told a thousand times to demonize his mother, but he didn't remember *her*. Which parts were true, and how much was exaggerated, he would never know. Did she love him? Would she ever come back for him? He wondered as darkness fell on his young life.

Peoria, Illinois, 1959

They were young and had to get married.

She came from a long line of Lithuanian Catholics.

He grew up in the Ozark hills around Harrison, Arkansas. Many of the houses had no indoor toilets or running water. After graduating from high school, he left to seek a job and his fortune. Nothing much was left to keep him in the Ozarks. His mom, a staunch Christian, had died in the hospital after gallbladder surgery. An air bubble had crept into her bloodstream through the old-fashioned glass IV. His father, a heavy drinker, died a couple of years later.

The young couple had dated only for a short time, but when she got pregnant, it was expected they would marry. At the time, there were no other options. The young man made an honest woman of her, and for that he was proud of himself. He had done the right thing. He worked hard to support the family.

⁂

Harrison, Arkansas, 1965

Confused and dazed, the boy woke up. *Where am I?* He groggily climbed out of bed and began to cry softly. *Where's 'Lizbeth?* The door opened, and a strange woman came in.

"Mommy! I want my mommy! Where's 'Lizbeth?"

"What's all this hollerin' about, Lonnie?" she said in a scratchy voice. "Now quiet yourself down. Mommy's not here. She's in Peoria. Elizabeth is already awake. She's in the kitchen."

The boy looked at her, his brown eyes wide. Her dark hair was piled high on her head, and her eyes, sunken in gray sockets, were businesslike and lonely. She smiled, crooked teeth and all.

"Why, ya don't know me, do ya?" She softened. "I'm your auntie, your daddy's sister-in-law." Auntie went on. "You're probably hungry, ain't ya? We've got some grits and corn bread." She coaxed the reluctant boy. "Come on. It'll be all right. You'll see. Get yourself dressed and come on out. We'll have us some breakfast."

Shaking, the boy began to pull on his jeans. He was frightened. He wanted his mommy and daddy. He wanted to leave this dingy room and go home. When he had finished dressing, he followed Auntie. Wandering through the living room, he noticed a stained, worn, green sofa; a chair; and a television.

He didn't have a television at home. The boy stopped to look at it. He wished he could turn it on and watch something. Then he heard his father.

"I just don't know what I'll do now. How can I raise two young'uns all by myself? I've gotta work. Who'll watch the kids?" A great moan was followed by heaving sobs.

"I just can't believe it. I'd be mighty upset too" a man's deep voice offered comfort. "It'll be all right. We'll think of something."

"She was in your bed with another man?" Auntie asked in her distinctive drawl. "What'd ya do?"

"I left and came back home to Arkansas, to James's house," Daddy said. "I didn't know what to do. I needed my big brother. I needed help, so I drove all the way down here."

"Why'd ya even stay with the whore?" Auntie pressed. "You telling me that she just run off with other men or slept with those men in your own bedroom?" She shook her head disapprovingly.

"I don't know. I just couldn't think—can't think. I don't know what to do now. I've got no place to live up there. I didn't show up for work the last three days, so I suppose I don't have a job to go back to." Daddy began to sob again, uncontrollably.

The boy wanted to run to him, to put his arms around him. He started toward his father, but Auntie grabbed his arm.

"No!"

He jumped at the sharpness of her tone and began to cry. "I want my daddy. Let me go. Let me go!" In anger, he fell to the floor screaming.

"Let him come. Come here, son."

She released her grip on his arm. The boy ran and flung his arms around his father's neck. He then crawled onto Daddy's lap at the table. Daddy cried harder.

Then he saw her—his little sister—sitting in a chair pulled close to the table. Her head barely rose over the edge. She just stared. Only three, she didn't understand, but she began to whine, "I want my mommy."

Auntie picked her up. "Elizabeth, Mommy's far away. She can't come right now."

The door opened, and another big man came in. The boy remembered: He's the man from last night—Big Brother, Daddy had called him. He was a great big man with chubby cheeks and wide shoulders. The boy liked Big Brother instantly.

"Well, looks like you survived that mess all right," Big Brother said. He looked down at the boy with tenderness and smiled. "You are a cute one, aren't you?" He tousled the boy's red hair.

The boy looked around and saw the other uncle who came with Big Brother and Daddy. Auntie said, "Oh, you children haven't been properly introduced. That there is your Uncle James," she pointed to Big Brother. "This other guy, he's Uncle Richard. He's my husband and your daddy's brother."

Uncle James took Elizabeth from Auntie's arms and held her close. The boy began to relax. Maybe these strange people weren't so bad.

Auntie began spooning grits and corn bread muffins onto plates. She placed a bowl and a muffin in front of the boy, and he suddenly realized he was hungry. He wanted to eat. He climbed off Daddy's lap, stood next to him and began nibbling his muffin. The little sister reached to get down, then went back to her chair at the table and ate too.

Daddy tried to talk about what happened before he left Peoria, but every time someone mentioned the name of Judy, the boy's mother, Daddy cried again.

"You wouldn't believe the mess those kids were in," Uncle Richard said. "When we got to Peoria, we went into the house. It was filthy. The kids were both locked in the bedroom in their cribs."

"The boy was in a crib?" Auntie interjected. "Why, he's way too big to be in a crib."

"That's not the worst of it. The worst is that she wasn't anywhere to be found. She wasn't in the yard. She wasn't in the kitchen. She was gone." A long pause ensued as he considered his next words. "The only people in the house were the kids. She left those kids all alone, she did."

"No!"

"We just had to take them, didn't we James? They had been alone for hours. Both had dirty, wet diapers on."

James nodded.

"They're too big to be wearing diapers. She hasn't potty trained them yet? What kind of mother was she?"

"We gave them a quick bath, packed their clothes in them sacks," he nodded toward some paper bags in the corner, "and then we just grabbed the kids, put them in the Chevy, and drove away."

The boy remembered later that his dad told him his mother called a couple days later. She just wanted to be sure he had the kids. She became a silent, unknown entity in his life—as if she had never existed except at family reunions, when this aunt or that aunt would comment, "Those poor kids." "They have no mommy." "She just left them."

3

Alienated

> You are…a people belonging to God, that you may declare the praises of him who called you out of darkness into his wonderful light.
>
> 1 PETER 2:9 NIV

Harrison, Arkansas, 1965

Some things in life call to children. They beckon like the wind whispering to the dying leaves on the old oak tree: touch me, hold me, and see how I move. For the boy, nothing spoke stronger or clearer than the shiny globe on the third shelf of Auntie's cabinet. The pretty glass ball sparkled like a rainbow. It was round except on the bottom, which was flattened so it wouldn't roll off the shelf. The globe glistened as bright, sunny rays bounced off its iridescent sphere of rainbow colors.

The boy had been warned that some things were beyond reach. He was not even to touch them. But temptation played across the developing circuits of the boy's brain. What would he do? How could he reach it? Thoughts of potential peril did not cross his mind.

He spied the stool and dragged it slowly across the floor, carefully pushing it into place directly beneath the shiny ball. The reason he was not allowed to touch the globe did not penetrate his thinking. It was as if the warning "Do not touch the globe" had never entered his memory bank.

Life was void of simple pleasures for the curious boy. He experienced no baseball games, trips to the park, or adventures in the woods. No neighbor children lived nearby: the closest house was about three miles away as the crow flies. There were no video games, books, or puzzles. It was a home for grown-ups.

To the outsider, it might seem that this boy had been deprived of his basic childlike nature. But when a person doesn't know what he is missing, it's irrelevant. Endless days of wandering a barren yard of mowed weeds soon wore his curiosity thin. Minus the occasional rattlesnake that slithered across the grass, the boy's excitement level was only slightly above his age on a scale of one to ten.

On this day, the enticing glass globe reflected the morning sun cutting through the dusty air and dancing amid dust particles. It would be a glorious day to be able to play with something so beautiful.

"I didn't mean it!"

"Doesn't matter, you little brat, you're gonna pay!" she screamed.

Tears spilled from the boy's eyes, and a muffled, throaty cry caught in his throat as the door slammed shut and the lock turned. The dark closet smelled of stale cigarettes and cheap perfume. He was a prisoner, utterly alone at five years of age.

A sense of disbelief crept into his mind. He tried the door: it wouldn't open. He searched for a light switch but found none. Darkness enveloped him like a deep, dark fog, so thick that his hand vanished in front of his face. Tears streamed down his face, and sobs began to rack his body. Soon fear gave way to a sense of pain and rage in the depths of the boy's being. An explosion of anger brought his fists and feet to pound relentlessly on the door.

His screams had the sound of hurt and betrayal as he bellowed to be released. "Let me out! Let me out!" Over and over he screamed. Suddenly he felt the door open, and he was free!

Pain exploded in a sharp sting as he felt the open hand rake across his mouth and nose.

"Shut your mouth boy, or you'll never get out of here. Every time you scream you'll stay another hour."

The door slammed shut, and again he was alone.

The minutes passed slowly as the boy explored his tiny prison. He felt cold and searched for something to give him warmth. A stale-smelling, hooded sweatshirt lay on the dirty floor. He gratefully slipped it on and slowly slid to the floor.

His stomach growled with hunger. Soon, however, a greater problem presented itself: he needed to go to the bathroom. Intolerable discomfort racked his body as he fought the natural urge to relieve himself. Eventually, unable to win the battle, he succumbed and wet himself.

Those who watch clocks become slaves to time. To those with no clock, and no comprehension of time, time becomes an effective teacher as one learns to listen in the darkness. At first, the boy had no understanding; only questions, pain, and an overwhelming sense of fear and aloneness. He sobbed quietly as he curled into a ball and prayed for sleep.

The highlight of the boy's week was when the clan piled into their Chevy pickup for the Sunday trek to the little country church. He happily sang songs, played silly games, and eagerly listened to stories about the heroes of the Bible. Whether it was Daniel in the lion's den; Rack, Shack, and Benny in the fiery furnace; or Queen Esther risking her life for her people; the boy was cheered by stories of a God who answers prayers. Whether he learned by osmosis, had an innate sense of genuine faith, or merely clung to a misguided hope, he believed that God answers those who call out to him.

When locked in a dark, cold closet, the solution to darkness was simple. Simpler, in fact, than the world outside, with its complexities and misunderstandings. So simple that even a five-year-old boy could understand it. If God could protect the heroes of the Bible, he would protect the boy too.

In the months that followed, when he was driven to the closet for a second, third, or even tenth occasion, time became friendlier as he sang songs and playacted the stories of his heroes. In a world sometimes dark and cold, the boy felt warmer knowing there was a God out there watching out for the Daniels locked in lions' dens…and closets.

4

Secure

> When God, our kind and loving Savior God, stepped in, he saved us from all that. It was all his doing; we had nothing to do with it.
> TITUS 3:5 MSG

Ottawa, Kansas, 1967

Every summer, the Flippo clan gathered for a family reunion. As usual, Winnie and Ed, the boy's biological aunt on his father's side and her husband, made plans to attend that summer. Word of the children's plight had spread quickly throughout the family, and Winnie felt a heaviness in her heart for them. They had lived with James and his wife for a year until she became pregnant. Then they went back to Anna and Richard's. Now Anna was pregnant. The children needed a permanent home. What was God's plan for these children? How could the family care for them?

After several years of marriage, Ed and Winnie wanted children yet remained childless. Winnie wanted Lonnie and Elizabeth but was afraid to voice her heart's desire. They needed her; she needed them. God had a plan for them, and she was convinced she was a part of it. Meanwhile, her husband was having his own struggle.

While in Arkansas with the family, Winnie mentioned to Ed that she wanted to help her niece and nephew, to take them in and give them a stable home. But Ed expressed concern about their unruly behavior.

"They're a mess," Ed declared, dismissing the notion of taking them in. They didn't speak of it again for several months.

One morning that fall, as the scent of fresh bacon, toast, and eggs filled the air, Ed sat down to breakfast. "I can't sleep," he announced. "God keeps waking me up. Every morning, I have one thought in my mind: Ed, if you don't help Lonnie and Beth, who will? I'll never sleep another night if we don't do something."

He paused before declaring: "Let's go get them this weekend."

Aunt Winnie and Uncle Ed lived in the small town of Ottawa in Kansas. There the boy had a home, food, and safety. He and his sister loved the farm, the animals, the fields, and the barns. They played in the hayloft, ran free, and, for the first time, laughed as children should. They even had their own dog and cat. When they walked to Great Aunt Gladys and Great Uncle Arthur's house up the road, their dog Chipper walked right beside them. It was a treat any child would relish. Gladys and Arthur gladly became the grandparents the children had never had.

The farm became a place to learn the value of hard work, to understand where food and sustenance came from. Because he had chores, the farm became his home.

The holes were filling, but the pain and separation and the sense of loss were, at times, more than the boy could bear—especially when nighttime came. Every night, at bedtime, he wondered why his parents had still not come to get him and his sister. He couldn't help himself: every night he secretly prayed they would come.

☙❧

Ottawa, Kansas, 1973

A few years later, as the boy and his sister sat down to dinner, Aunt Winnie said she had great news: she was going to have a baby! The two children looked at each other with questioning expressions. They said nothing.

After dinner they went to the boy's room. "We'll have to move again," Beth said. "First Aunt Fern got pregnant and we had to go. Then Aunt Anna got pregnant and we came here. Now Aunt Winnie is pregnant. Will they send us back to Harrison?"

"No!" the boy blurted. "We're going to run away. We'll pack our bags and run away. We're not going back!"

In the weeks that followed, the boy and his sister made their plans and packed bags that they hid under the bed. One day, after dinner, Aunt Winnie and Uncle Ed asked the children to sit on the sofa in the living room.

Beth's teacher had called. Beth had written an essay about why she and her brother were going to have to move again and were instead planning to run away. She was worried about the impact the baby would have on the children.

"Beth and Lonnie, you know we want you here, right?" Winnie asked.

"I guess so."

Beth just stared straight ahead.

"You won't have to go anywhere after this baby is born." She placed her hand on her enlarged belly. "Kids, this is your home. Isn't it Ed?"

Ed nodded.

The boy looked at his sister and smiled slightly, tentatively. She, now eleven, looked relieved. He had no idea how Aunt Winnie knew, but she understood they were afraid the baby meant they would have to leave—and neither she nor Uncle Ed wanted them to go.

The boy went to his room and unpacked the bag he had hidden under his bed. Slowly, like the wind blowing over a golden wheat field, a notion was settling over him: His parents weren't coming back to get him. He was growing up. But here with Aunt Winnie and Uncle Ed, he finally had a place to call home.

5

Lonely

The people who walked in darkness have seen a great light.
Isaiah 9:2 msg

Harrison, Arkansas, 1965

James looked out the window and sighed. As the oldest in the family, he felt it was his duty to watch over his brothers and sisters since Mom and Dad had died. One, in particular, desperately needed his help. His brother sat alone under the oak tree, muttering softly to himself. Marion's two children, Lonnie and Betsy, were up the road at another brother's home.

James slipped down on the dry, crunchy grass beside Marion. For a long time, neither said anything.

"I need help, James," Marion said finally. "I ain't right. I'm like a mad dog that needs to be put down. I'm angry and so sad."

※

Ottawa, Kansas, 1970

"Kids, we're going on a trip today," Aunt Winnie announced.

"Where to? How long?" Beth asked eagerly.

"What for?" they wanted to know.

"We're going to see your daddy, about a hundred miles away," Winnie answered.

"Our daddy?" Beth began singing happily, "We're going to see Daddy, we're going to see Daddy..."

"Our dad?" the boy asked without emotion.

"Yes, your dad, Lonnie!" Ed confirmed.

"I thought we couldn't see him," the boy stated flatly.

"Well, that has changed, so we're going."

※

Nevada, Missouri, 1970

The smell of ether and antiseptic hung heavily in the air as the young boy and his family crept gingerly down the hallway.

Everywhere he looked, he saw strangeness. One man slowly banged his head softly against the wall while another cried softly, over and over, "I didn't do it, I didn't do it."

Lonely

Farther down, a woman reached for the children. "My pets, come to me," she said, her eyes grossly huge in the dim light.

It scared the boy and his little sister, and they clung tightly to each other. They moved through the halls pretending that they were invisible to those around them.

The person they had come to visit sat alone in the cheap wooden chair, a blank stare on his haggard face. He was unshaven, and his blond hair hung sloppily across listless eyes.

"Go ahead," his uncle whispered. "Go say hi."

"I'm not going," his sister cried, clinging to Aunt Winnie. The boy shuffled toward the man, shoulders hunkered, head down, and stood quietly in front of him.

Slowly the man's head tilted upright; his eyes fought to focus. He struggled through a drug-induced haze to look at his son.

"Hi, Daddy." The boy spoke, but he was unable to look into the man's face or meet his gaze. It was Daddy, but it wasn't Daddy. Something was wrong.

"Hello, son," his father slurred. "How's my little man?"

⁂

They drove away, the boy's aunt crying softly in the front seat. Her husband laid his hand on hers and promised, "Don't worry, we'll never bring them—or you—here again."

"It's so sad. I had no idea."

Looking back, the boy saw the sign. He had missed it when they drove in. Bright red rose bushes adorned the bottom, and shiny yellow words with blue trim stood out.

"Auntie, what does 'mentally ill' mean?" he asked. Receiving no answer, he slowly gave in to sleep; the only sound in his ears was that of his aunt's soft crying.

True to his uncle's word, the boy and his sister never returned to visit their father at the hospital, but the unease he felt that day never left him.

Ottawa, Kansas, 1972

Like any other day, the boy slowly rode his banana-seat bike down the dusty road to the white farmhouse where he lived. But on this day, he saw an unfamiliar blue car in the driveway.

"Your daddy is here," Aunt Winnie announced.

"Hi, son."

"Hi, Daddy. Are you going back to that hospital?"

"No son, I'm out, and I'll never go back again."

"I'm glad," said the boy.

"Thank you, son," said the father. "You saved my life."

"How did I do that, Daddy?"

"After you visited, I decided you would never have to come and see me there again. I got better, so I got out."

"I'm glad, Daddy, 'cause Sissy and I didn't like that place."

"Neither did I, son." The father hugged his boy. "Neither did I."

His father was a silent shadow who came and went from time to time. Others raised the boy while his father lived at the institution for years. When he was released, he watched the teenagers become adults from the sidelines. The boy's sense of loss, growing up without his father, was suffocating. A cavernous, dark hole in his soul ached with anger, frustration, loneliness, and resentment. He never understood the source of his inability to forgive others, to connect with those who loved him.

Sometimes life denies us understanding. Like a tree falling in an empty forest, no one is there to hear. It may appear that God himself is silent. No answer emerges. In those times, the boy learned to listen to the silence.

6

Frightened

> You'll do best by filling your mind and meditating on things true.
> PHILIPPIANS 4:8 MSG

Ottawa, Kansas, 1970

Darkness enveloped the room. Like a thick, heavy cloud, it covered his face—so deep, so heavy, and so stifling. The boy passed his hand in front of his face and saw nothing. At that moment, it seemed like darkness and silence were his constant companions.

Earlier that week, as they moved his furniture and clothing downstairs, it seemed like a great idea to have his own room in the basement. He loved the idea in daylight, when there were no shadows. He felt big and grown up. He was now ten! But the first night sleeping alone in his new room in the basement wasn't turning out quite as he had planned.

The boy lay awake, unable to sleep. Suddenly he heard a noise outside his door. He crept over and tried to listen over the sound of his heartbeat throbbing in his head.

His throat swelled shut as a lump rose from his chest and forced its way toward his mouth. He had no doubt that he was not alone. Someone or something was under the staircase in the basement!

Conjured images terrorized the boy's mind as he recalled the magazine he had looked at earlier that day. On the cover was the ugliest witch he had ever seen, stirring a boiling cauldron in a basement.

He had known better than to look at that magazine. He not only hated horror stories, he was scared to death of them. Why he had looked was beyond his own understanding. Was it the thrill of the moment? A craving for an adrenaline rush? Peer pressure? He couldn't explain why he had looked, but he had. Now it brought back tormenting memories of darkness and loneliness.

Images of zombies, blood squirting from chopped-off limbs, and people screaming flashed through his memory. It seemed like only yesterday. He was back in Arkansas, in the backseat of the Chevy, watching horror movies while their guardians ate popcorn and M&M's. His sister, four, buried her head in his shoulder and sobbed quietly while he stroked her hair and told her not to look.

His emotions now were the same as when he'd been in that car, but this time he was in a dark basement, and a witch was in the next room with only a flimsy wooden door between them. Bile rose in his mouth, and tears slid down his face. Mustering every ounce of his strength, he threw open the door and raced up the steps to the first floor. Wrenching open the latch, he ran through the doorway as fast as he could fly. Making rapidly for his aunt and uncle's room, he pounded on their door as great sobs of fear wracked his body.

Immediately he felt caring, loving arms around him. Finally feeling safe and secure, he wept hysterically, broken and devastated, even as the fear vanished.

"What happened, Lonnie? Why are you so scared?" his uncle asked.

"I saw scary things." The boy explained about the magazine, the horror movies from years ago, and what he feared was under the stairs outside his basement bedroom.

"Oh, son, witches are not real in that way," Winnie said. "But these fears are the result of what you read today. What you put in your mind affects you."

"Sleep up here with us tonight on the floor," Ed said. "You'll be safe."

His voice betrayed no scorn or disappointment. The boy learned that night that what the eye has seen and the heart embraces can leave scars.

7

Determined

> Keep it up, and don't let anyone intimidate or silence you.
> ACTS 18:9 MSG

San Jose, California, 2010

The buzz of a bee; the clouds floating silently above the rolling hills; flowers of radiant colors, small trees, bushes, and weeds sprinkle the landscape of the man's heightened senses on a hot summer day. As he sits on the park bench, he concurrently feels a sense of strength and smallness. The wind sweeps through the trees, refreshing his face with cool bursts of hope. His life unfolds before him like the valleys and peaks of the hills of Santa Teresa Park. His life. His hopes. His dreams. He is a man whose life is more than half over.

Yet he still dreams. Even at this late stage, he has hopes for his career, marriage, and family. He wonders why he can still dream when others his age are frantically grasping for something intangible, running away from responsibility, relationships, and careers.

Then he remembers a baseball game years ago.

⁂

Ottawa, Kansas, 1970

In the profoundly scorching days of a Kansas summer, a boy's spirit soars with dreams or droops like parched grass. It began the summer of 1970 on the baseball field at Orlis Cox Complex. The boy was nine years old. For the past two seasons, he and his buddies had played Little League baseball on the peewee fields—open diamonds without fences. But that year they moved to the big field, complete with a scoreboard and fences. Anyone who hit a home run over the fence in our small farm town became a baseball hero—the George Brett of Ottawa. More than anything, the boy wanted his over-the-fence home run to be marked with white chalk on that old green-and-gold wooden scoreboard. He daydreamed about it.

Baseball was his passion. He lived to feel the sand and dirt rub his pants brown as he slid into home plate, to hear the crack of the ball on wood, and to feel the smack of leather ball hitting leather glove as he caught fly balls and line drives. He longed to touch second and throw to first for a double play. That was what he dreamed about in his ninth summer.

Like most naive kids, the boy just had to tell someone his dream. After practice, he rode his bike home, washed his hands, and sat down to a dinner of fried chicken at the farm table. He anticipated his aunt and uncle's reaction: they would encourage him and say, "You can do it, Lonnie!" He waited for the right moment—a moment of silence, or when one of his guardians would ask him about his day. The meal seemed excruciatingly long as his sister whined about having to eat her peas and carrots.

"Lonnie, what did you do today?" his uncle asked. "I saw you riding home with your glove and bat."

"Today we practiced on the big field," he said excitedly. "I hit the ball way out in the field. Someday, I want to hit a home run over the fence!"

"Humph," his uncle snorted.

His aunt said nothing to him, continuing instead to encourage Betsy to eat the hated vegetables.

The boy had been told many times throughout his young life that he couldn't have certain things. "No, you cannot have that new bike. We can't afford it."

"No pie for you, young man."

"You don't need new jeans. You have two pairs."

"Why do you need your own radio?"

He had not put the pieces together until that moment. In his young mind, the only thing he heard was: "You're dreaming, kid. You can't do that." He interpreted his uncle's "Humph" as yet another big, fat NO. Stifling silence enveloped him.

In that moment, something within him rose up in defiance, anger, and determination. He was going to hit a home run—if for no other reason, just to prove to them that he could. Somehow, all his life dreams seemed wrapped up in hitting a home run. If he didn't hit a home run that summer, he just knew that the silence of invisibility would never end. He was afraid he would never realize his dreams.

His uncle's belief that hitting a home run over the fence was beyond the boy's ability fanned a flame that altered the boy's perspective like a fire changes the landscape. Rather than giving up or drying up under the lack of support, raging frustration was transformed into a controlled burn.

Just weeks later, the boy dragged his left foot across the white chalk line and set his right foot. Lightly twisting his front cleat, he readied his body and mind for the pitch.

Crack!

As the ball sailed across the fence for a home run, the boy raced from first base to second without slowing down.

"Slow down, son," the umpire said, grinning. "It's a home run. Enjoy it. Awesome hit!"

His teammates mobbed him at home plate, and he heard the chant: "Grand slam! Grand slam! Grand slam!"

For the first time, the boy realized that he had not only hit his first out-of-the-park homer, but it was the best possible kind of home run to boot—a grand slam!

As other kids climbed into their cars with their families and left the park, the boy pedaled his bike across the parking lot, alone. He was used to it. His aunt and uncle were eking out a living working the fields and couldn't take time to watch him play.

Reveling in the joy and glory of the moment, the new George Brett of Ottawa slowly rode his bicycle home. He had more than accomplished his dream. He couldn't wait to tell his family!

※

Like the slap of an open hand across his face, the reality of his uncle's words struck harder than his bat had hit the ball: "Why are you lying about hitting a home run? It's pitiful that you have to resort to such lies to get attention."

Like hot drops of molten lead, tears dripped from the boy's eyes and his face flashed red. "I am not lying!" he screamed. He stormed from the table and ran crying into the oppressive night.

The boy and his uncle did not speak of the incident the next day—or the next—and it appeared forgotten. But the pain and hurt settled deeper into the boy's spirit. Not having his family there to share his moment of triumph was one thing, but that they didn't even believe he had done it cut sharply into his heart. If even his family denied that his dreams could come true—that they had come true—would society deny and reject him as well?

Two days later, the boy rode with his uncle to the Firestone tire shop. Nothing broke the silence in the cab of the 1965 Chevrolet truck.

When they walked into the Firestone store, a chorus of customers seemed anxious to greet them. "There's the man!" one nodded at the boy and smiled.

"What a blast!" said another, clearly impressed. Then he addressed the boy's dumbfounded uncle: "You sure must be proud…and a grand slam to boot!"

"That Lonnie is quite a ballplayer!"

On the way back to the farm, neither the boy nor his uncle spoke. But when he turned into the driveway and turned off the engine, the uncle offered these wise words: "I'm sorry I didn't believe you, Lonnie. I was wrong. Keep dreaming your dreams, and don't let anyone—and I mean anyone—kill your dreams."

His uncle gave the boy a gift that day: empowerment. The words *keep dreaming* empowered the boy to dream more, to dream bigger, to never to give up.

That's why he was able to sit on a park bench years later, with his life more than half over, and still have excitement for the future, to create new dreams with his wife, to hope for a better tomorrow, and to soar to new heights of achievement and fulfillment.

8

Angry

> Little choices in life make big differences in the long term.
> LON W. FLIPPO

Ottawa, Kansas, 1972
The crowd roars as he steps to the plate—some in fear, others in approval. A runner stands at second, two outs, bottom of the ninth, two strikes. Although his team is losing, he represents the tying run. The pitcher grins, mocking; starts his windup at the mound, and delivers the pitch.
  CRACK!

Like a car on a pleasant drive screeching to a halt at sudden danger, the boy was jolted from his daydream when he heard the cry—a cry of pain and fear. In an instant, the situation crystallized in his mind. His baby sister was being tormented by the neighborhood bully. In a flash, his pleasant daydream was replaced with thoughts of vengeance.

Moments later, stick in hand, he thrashed the tormentor's bare bottom. A brief feeling of regret crossed his mind, but the cry of fear from his sister echoed through his mind, urging him on. He heard the smack of wood on skin as he dragged the broken willow tree across flesh, and it almost seemed as though someone else were holding the stick.

He digs in at the plate and focuses on the pitcher's hand as he delivers the fastball. The bat feels stiff, yet flexible, in his hand. The coarse wood digs into his soft palms. This is the moment. He prepares to deliver the game-winning blow.

The boy was slammed back to reality by a high-pitched scream and the click of metal. "I'm gonna kill you!" a girl screamed, squarely pointing a double-barreled shotgun at his face. "Don't ever touch my brother again, or I will end you, boy!"

The shotgun was elongated, with gold emblems and a strong steel trigger; the girl's hands trembled under the weight of the weapon as she slowly cocked the hammer. The boy froze. He stared down the gaping barrels of the menacing shotgun. If she chose to pull that trigger, he had absolutely no doubt he would die.

When one faces death, he gains new perspective. Small decisions, opinions, and preferences—like whether to drink

Coke or Pepsi—suddenly seem frivolous. In that instant, the young boy knew that his seemingly small decision to whip the boy who had tormented his sister had caught up to him. Now his entire existence depended on the decision of this girl.

The shiny hickory stick with the black, Louisville Slugger logo feels strong in his hands. The crack of the ball meeting wood reverberates through his body and mind as the rawhide rockets into right center field. Rounding first base, he breaks for second, and then faces the moment of truth. Should he try for third or stay at second? With a quick glimpse, he sees the lead runner crossing home plate. His third-base coach is signaling for him to stop, but the boy ignores him. Without breaking stride, he streaks for third base. The throw darts toward the bag. He slides, trying to beat it.

"You're out!"

The game is over. The extra effort is too much, the attempt more than what was wise. He'd failed.

When the boy came to himself, he was alone on the gravel road, walking toward home. He was alive, but he had no recollection of what had happened or how he had escaped.

The daydream was over.

⸺⸻⸺

Springfield, Missouri, 1991
Years later, living in Missouri with his wife and new daughter, the man couldn't believe the risk he had taken on that day in

Ottawa, Kansas. A sense of guilt and grace filled his soul. Was it an act of mercy that he still breathed after that shocking moment or just a tragic mistake? His daughter would not be here if the girl had pulled the trigger.

That day had changed him. He learned an important lesson: violence, whether born in rage or righteous vengeance, would, in the end, hurt him as well as others. There would always be a reckoning for doing things his way.

9

Guilty

> We need friends going in the right direction.
>
> Lon W Flippo

Ottawa, Kansas, 1974

His dad was president of a college. He lived in the richest neighborhood. He was good-looking, athletic, and his sister was a cheerleader—and gorgeous. Who wouldn't want David as his best friend?

The boy thought David was one of the coolest kids in junior high, and for some unexplained reason, he chose him to be his best friend. Through pizza parties, sleepovers, and just hanging out, the two boys quickly became inseparable.

One fall day, after school, the boys were riding their bikes home when David said casually, "Hey, I've got something to show you."

"Sure, sounds great," the boy replied. "What is it?"

"You'll see."

The gravel crackled under bicycle wheels as the boys rode down a path toward a hidden maintenance shed.

"Wait till you see this!" David boasted.

The window was dirty and covered with cobwebs. A brand-new bike with a yellow banana seat stood just inside the window, gleaming like a ray of sunlight.

"Wow!" The boy whistled softly.

"Exactly. What a beauty."

A moment of silence hung in the air like a hot-air balloon at the county fair.

"Here's what I'm thinking," said David. "We break out this window, you crawl in and unlock the door, and then we take the bike and sell it at school for fifty bucks."

The boy felt the air rush from his lungs like oxygen sucked from a room by a devouring fire. "What did you say?"

"Come on," David pressed. "I'll split the money with you fifty-fifty. Think of how many pinball games you can play and how much pizza you can eat at Pizza Village with twenty-five dollars!"

The boy's mind raced.

"If I know the law but still can't keep it, and if the power of sin within me keeps sabotaging my best intentions, I obviously need help! I realize that I don't have what it takes. I can will

it, but I can't do it. I decide to do good, but I don't really do it; I decide not to do bad, but then I do it anyway. My decisions, such as they are, don't result in actions. Something has gone wrong deep within me and gets the better of me every time" (Romans 7:17–20 MSG).

The boy knew the right thing to do, but losing David's approval and friendship was something he was not willing to risk—he worshiped David. He knew it was dangerous. He knew it was wrong. But he followed David down the thieving trail.

A few days later, "Pinball Wizard," the hit song by Elton John, blasted on the jukebox at Pizza Village. The boy stroked the flippers on the pinball machine, guzzled Pepsi, and stuffed down pieces of thin-crust, hamburger-and-mushroom pizza. Life felt charged. He loved the adrenaline rush of his newfound activities.

Over the next few months, the "Ice Finger Boys," as they dubbed themselves, pilfered everything from LP records and pornographic magazines to cigarettes and electronics. If it was considered contraband or expensive, the boys stole it and sold it at school. Requests to purchase the stolen goods poured in from fellow students as David and the boy's reputation for dealing on the black market spread. Money could be made, and they were going to get it. The boy quickly discovered that the thrill of stealing was in his blood and could not be tamed. He wanted more. From grocery stores to convenience stores, from churches to homes, he and David incessantly sought the next score, the next adrenaline rush.

They carefully planned and executed most of their thefts. One boy would act as decoy while the other seized whatever illicit items were the target that day. They stuffed merchandise down their underwear, jammed it under jackets, and wedged it into newspaper bags. The cover for their thievery was their paper routes. The large, empty newspaper bags the boys carried after they finished their deliveries obscured their hands. The few remaining papers concealed the items filched from drug stores, groceries, and gas stations.

Soon that grew old, and the boys sought other means to feed their growing obsession with larceny. They contrived a way to steal while collecting payments for the newspaper. While waiting for payment at the door, it was easy to spot merchandise and money in homes.

"You boys come in out of the cold. I'll get you some money." Mrs. Johnson shuffled to her bedroom to get her purse.

David quickly motioned for his friend to trail her steps and spy out where she hid her money. Watching her reach under her pillow, the boy saw Mrs. Johnson pull a roll of bills out and peel a few off for paying the boys. Quickly slinking back down the hall, the boy joined David at the door and smiled at Mrs. Johnson as she returned.

"Here's a little something extra for you boys," she said kindly. "Thank you for putting the paper in my screen door so I don't have to walk down those slippery steps."

"You're welcome, Mrs. Johnson," the boys chimed in unison.

"Bye, now," the boy added. "Have a nice afternoon."

The plan was simple: the boy knew where the stash was, so he would go in while David acted as a decoy. David would knock on the front door and ask for help, pretending to be sick. The boy would sneak in the back door that Mrs. Johnson always kept unlocked for her cat. While they were occupied on the porch, the boy would steal the roll of money.

Three days later, adrenaline surged through the boy's body as he waited for David to lure the old woman to the porch.

Why am I doing this? The boy asked himself. For the money? For David's friendship? What's next after this?

In his heart and head, he knew better. He was better than this; he knew right from wrong.

"It happens so regularly that it's predictable. The moment I decide to do good, sin is there to trip me up. I truly delight in God's commands, but it's pretty obvious that not all of me joins in that delight. Parts of me covertly rebel, and just when I least expect it, they take charge. I've tried everything and nothing helps. I'm at the end of my rope. Is there no one who can do anything for me? Isn't that the real question?" (Romans 7:21–24 MSG).

The scriptures Uncle Ed had read aloud the previous night during family devotions came back to the boy's mind. Yet, amazingly, his fingers still closed tightly around the wad of money as he crept back down the hall, through the kitchen, and out the back door.

He split $600 with David that day. It was the biggest take of their delinquent careers. Nothing ever happened. The boys were never questioned. Nobody ever found out. They got away clean, except for the boy's conscience, which triggered warning bells in his spirit. Yet again he ignored them and chased the rush that breaking the law—and friendship with David—delivered.

A few weeks later, the boy was in Briscoe's drugstore, buying candy and gum. At the checkout counter, the owner of the store said, "That will be eighty-nine cents for the candy and $49.95 for the radio in your bag."

The boy felt the man's eyes lock onto his reddening face. "What did you say?" he stammered.

"That will be $49.95…or should I call the cops?"

"What if I just give it back to you and walk away?"

"That will be fine too, but don't ever come back here again, or I will call the police."

Later, as the teenage boy replayed the incident in his head, he concluded that he was lucky: he wasn't getting booked for theft at the police station. A tear slid down his cheek. What a mess he had made of things. What a fool he had become.

That evening Aunt Winnie and Uncle Ed asked the boy to talk with them after supper. From time to time, his guardians sat him down for such talks—when he had done something wrong. He wondered what he'd done this time. Dread crept into his mind. Did they know about the thefts? How could they? No, he reassured himself, it was probably just another attitude-adjustment talk. It had to be. Anxiously, he waited for them to speak. The silence hung like burned sulfur in the air as he waited for them to speak.

"We've noticed a change in you," Uncle Ed finally said. "You have more money than usual. You're coming home late from your paper route. Something is different since you started hanging around with David."

They knew! Warning bells sounded in the boy's brain. His heart began to beat faster.

"Sometimes our friends can get us off track," Aunt Winnie began. "David comes from a good family, but he's on a different path than is right for you. We don't see him as a good influence. Please consider cutting down the time you spend with him."

That was it? That's all? The boy's initial reaction was overwhelming relief. As he lay awake in bed that night, however, he realized that his aunt and uncle did know. How could they know that David's friendship was pulling him into darkness? He was surprised how well they understood his relationship with David without really knowing the details.

As he pondered what his aunt and uncle had said, the boy had a revelation: David was not with him when he had attempted to steal the radio from the drugstore. The truth began to sink in. He had become something he didn't want to be. It was no longer David's influence driving his behavior. He alone had made that choice. He was the one stealing, and he could no longer blame anyone but himself.

A path of destruction lay before him. For the first time, he saw it clearly. If unchecked, he would get caught and be arrested. His future would be limited by a police record. Worse yet, he might lose what he craved most: freedom.

In the weeks that followed, with firm resolve, the boy began to distance himself from his best friend. They parted amicably. It wasn't easy, but the boy found new friends. Stealing became a thing of the past—illustrations to tell his own children when they struggled to do right, or to share with other children who had similar choices to make.

———

The boy never understood why David's friendship had meant so much to him. In moments of reflection, he considered where David's path ended. One day David walked into a store and, instead of candy, he wanted cash, and instead of using a newspaper bag, he pulled a gun. The arrest was his third, so in his mid-twenties, a judge sentenced him to thirty years in prison for armed robbery.

If not for the grace of God, family, and the Briscoe drugstore manager, the boy knew that he, too, would be sitting in prison.

10

Tempted

> No more stumbling around. Get on with it!
>
> EPHESIANS 5:8 MSG

Ottawa, Kansas, 1976

The puff of smoke rose slowly into the summer sky. It was a hot, humid day in eastern Kansas. The small creek that meandered through the woods was slowly changing from a stream into murky pools of algae-laden water.

The boy pulled a drag from the cigarette in his hand. He was sixteen, alone, hiding, and smoking his first cigarette. Many people in his family were smokers; at family reunions, massive plumes of nicotine-laden clouds covered the area where they congregated. As kids, the boy and his sister would race through the crowd of adults dispersing the fumes as though Superman were parting the clouds. Later, as elementary-aged masters of knowledge, they were careful where they ran and walked, so as to avoid the mucus-covered balls of crud that different aunts and uncles coughed up.

The boy knew better than to smoke. His aunt and uncle didn't smoke, and he had heard the health hazards of smoking many times. But there he was, cigarette in hand and the taste of nicotine and tar on his lips. He mimicked his TV and movie heroes as he slowly pulled on the small stick and watched the tobacco leaves burn. Mesmerized, he carefully blew the smoke from his mouth so he would not inhale and cough up his own hideous, mucus-covered ball of crud. His mind drifted as he knelt down in the creek bed and gazed up into the cloudless sky.

A slight movement registered in his peripheral vision. Turning his head, he saw a snake. Having grown up on a farm, he knew a copperhead when he saw it. It seemed to appear from nowhere, like the serpent in the Garden of Eden. The poisonous snake—it looked to be about three feet long—was coiled up and hiding in the washed-out roots of the tree. Its forked tongue flickered slowly in and out as it tested the air for any sign of danger. Its beady eyes frozen, the snake was a mere two feet from the young man's face. It almost appeared to be speaking to the young smoker.

Trying desperately to recall his outdoor scout training, the boy remained frozen. The smoke curled from the cigarette and drifted casually up into his face. He was a good mile from home, and alone: a bite in the face or neck could be fatal. Every instinct in him screamed to run but he remained frozen. Thoughts of desperation and regret crossed his mind: Why am I out here smoking a stupid cigarette? Am I gonna die for a piece of tobacco? Consciousness of time and perception of reality beyond his own body and that of the snake faded as he focused completely on surviving.

Every person comes to a time of crisis, when he or she cries out to God and promises all kinds of things if only God will save him or her. He promises to sell all his possessions, become a missionary, or quit smoking. This was one of those times for the boy.

"Get me out of here. Please get me out of here. Help me! I'll do anything if you'll just help get me out of here. I'm gonna make it right…tonight. Tonight."

It seemed like forever, but it was only about thirty seconds later that the copperhead slowly turned and slithered away. After a moment of reflection, the young man extinguished his first—and last—cigarette.

Temptation to do wrong often passes beyond human understanding. The young man knew he shouldn't smoke, yet it seemed impossible to resist smoking that day. He knew smoking was a terrible, costly, dangerous habit; yet he fell headlong into the same enticement as those before him. Was it the sins of the father or mother revisited on the son? Was it simply his desire to be a man?

The momentary pleasure and excitement of giving in to desire were immediately abandoned in the presence of danger. He came to his senses. Why would he want to smoke anyway, and cough away his days and nights?

Like a peace offering, the boy carefully placed the pack of smokes into the roots of the tree as he prepared to leave. As his experiment in adult pleasure came to an end, the boy decided to steer clear of deadly snakes—and Camels.

11

Released

If you have anything against someone, forgive.
MARK 11:25 MSG

Grand Rapids, Michigan, 1979
The boy, now a young man, spoke little as he and his college buddy drove up the highway, exited in Grand Rapids, and followed the map to her home. The lump in his throat became larger each time they turned a corner. Is my mother beautiful? Old and wrinkled? Will she hug me and say, "I'm sorry"? His mind raced from one thought to another.

The car stopped. He climbed out and looked up at the faded siding on the old house that appeared to have been converted into apartments. He climbed the steps to the door, read the names, and debated. Every muscle in his body ached to turn around and run. He found the right apartment. He stood at the door a long time before he knocked. The last time he saw his mother, he was not even five, some fourteen or fifteen years ago.

The door opened. Immediately the scent of smoke and mold wafted to his nostrils. He tried not to react.

"You must be Lonnie," a petite woman said. She was thin. He could tell that she had once been beautiful and vivacious. Her features reminded him of his sister. This must be his mother, or at least an aunt.

"I'm your mother."

There was an awkward silence. She invited him in and opened the door all the way. She guided him to a seat on the blue sofa in the living room. "Tea? Coffee? Soda?" she offered as she sat in an adjacent chair and leaned forward.

"No, thank you," the boy replied as she sat on the sofa facing him.

"Your hair's not as red as I remember."

"Yeah, it's gotten less bright over the years."

"Well, I guess…" her voice trailed off as she looked away. "I offered to come and visit you about six years ago. Your aunt said you two were finally settling in and had a normal life now. She said if I came I had to stay in your lives for good. She said it wasn't a good time to alleviate my guilt at your expense. She was right.

"I did the best I could," she continued. "I was young. I didn't know how to care for two children. I was lonely."

"I understand," the boy replied, though he didn't.

Green Bay, Wisconsin, 1983

The boy, now a man, called to get his mother's address. He sent a wedding invitation. He phoned. She said she would come. She asked if his father was coming. "Yes," the boy told her. He made arrangements to give her a place of honor, but his Aunt Winnie would be positioned as the mother of the groom. His Uncle Ed was positioned as father of the groom, though his father was present and would be given a place of honor.

His mother didn't show up.

The boy married the woman of his dreams. It was the happiest day of his life thus far.

Atlanta, Georgia, 1992

The boy was now a husband with a young daughter and a son on the way. His chosen career was to be a children's pastor. He and five pastors on staff at the Carmel, Indiana, church were traveling to Georgia for a minister's conference. Driving down to Atlanta in a van with his coworkers, he could not have known that something was about to finally break the silence of abandonment for him.

As the worship service began, thousands of male voices sang in unison. The sight was stunning and moving for the young father. As the first speaker got up to share, a flood of light shone on a piece of the boy's spirit formerly hidden in the darkness of that closet from long ago. He hated his auntie. He was angry with his mother for not coming to get him. He had rage toward his father for not being strong enough to care for him. All that anger and frustration was hurting him and his young family.

The speaker talked about forgiving others who had no remorse. He said the only one hurt by unforgiveness is the unforgiving person and the people he or she loves most. God wants us to let it go. That evening, as tears poured down his cheeks, the boy was able to let it go; to weep for his lost childhood and begin the long journey of forgiving his mother and his father for not being able to take care of him; to appreciate what his aunt and uncle had so lovingly sacrificed to give him and his sister a stable home.

In the twenty years of silence preceding that evening in Atlanta—with no definitive word from his mother, his father, or God—he had wondered, Is God there? Does he care? Did he care about me as a boy? If he did, why did my parents forget about me?

In this briefest of moments, he knew God cared enough to give him a place to call home as a child, a place from which to begin his journey of forgiveness and life. He accepted that gift. He knew God loved him enough to give him a home with his wife and a career to share his gift of compassion for hurting children and families.

12

Hopeful

> I have it all planned out—plans to take care of you, not abandon you,
> plans to give you the future you hope for.
> JEREMIAH 29:11 MSG

Down the hill the automobile careened as its mechanical mass and the gravitational pull of the slope combined to create a force of destruction. Twiddling with the radio dial, the driver's attention was diverted from the road.

Around the next bend, the driver could not see the doe and her two fawns meandering slowly across the meadow toward the road. To graze on the lush grass across the ravine, they would have to cross the asphalt.

The man who was no longer a boy sat on a picnic table at the top of the hill, silently observing the beautiful deer.

Suddenly he heard the approaching car. His panic grew as he watched helplessly what seemed destined to unfold. Too far away to intervene, he could only watch, pray, and hope that life would be spared.

Head down, the driver continued on his course. It seemed nothing would stop the collision. The machine would be damaged, but flesh would be destroyed.

He was reminded of how society had become a self-perpetuating cycle of money and technology. It seems that those unwilling to join the perpetual motion will be destroyed—or certainly scarred for life—unless they find safety and shelter.

Fortunately, the protective mother deer was vigilant. She looked up and realized the approaching danger to her fawns. Maternal instinct kicked in: she quickly nudged her fawns, and together they bolted safely away.

Oblivious to his surroundings, the driver continued heedlessly down the road, unaware of the tragedy narrowly avoided.

The man realized that, like the doe, he was now a parent. It was his responsibility to provide safety and shelter, to protect the minds and spirits of his children, to nurture and love them and give them a place to call home. And with joy, he knew that although life had dealt him a hand devoid of face cards, God had given him the strength to become the master and captain of his life.

PART 2

Life Lessons for Parents

I grew up on a farm on the windy plains of Kansas. Each spring, we hooked the seeder behind the old Allis-Chalmers tractor and set out for the fields. From dawn till dusk, and sometimes past dark, my uncle plowed and dropped seeds in perfect row after perfect row.

Soon tender strands of soybean plants peaked through the soil. To me the rows were beautiful, but to the trained eye of my uncle, the soil was teeming with setbacks.

Beneath the surface, cockleburs often took root. When grown, the round seeds of that plant stuck to clothing or fur like superglue to fingers. The scratchy things snagged jeans and brought yelps when we removed them from old Skipper, our faithful dog.

Cockleburs grow quickly. Without prompt intervention, the vines intertwine with the plants and block the sun from reaching the beans; the soybean plants wither and produce scrawny fruit. So my uncle and I diligently checked the fields for cockleburs.

Like a soybean field, children must be diligently checked and nurtured if they are to mature into healthy, responsible adults. As parents, we tend to focus on mental and social development. But there are sinister "weeds" that can choke a child's spirit and prevent faith from growing.

Practicing these principles I learned from my aunt and uncle and from the parenting school of hard knocks can help prevent a child's spirit from being choked by life's cockleburs.

LESSON 1

Children Need a Place to Call Home

My healing did not end the day I arrived in Ottawa, Kansas, at my aunt and uncle's farm; it began there. To many, home is a house. But through the years I've come to believe that home, for a child, is the place where seeds of confidence can grow. For that to happen, home must have a combination of the following characteristics:

Freedom from Ridicule
A child's spirit withers when he or she is compared to others—siblings, other children, or even a parent. Kids needs to know

that they are important, loved, and valued no matter what they do, say, or look like. Comparisons leave all humans with a sense of failure to measure up.

Love and Acceptance

To children, home is where they are loved and accepted for who they are—flaws and all. Love is not a payout for performance. Even when a child throws a tantrum at the store or says a naughty word, he must know beyond a shadow of a doubt that his parents love and accept him.

Shelter

Home is the place where a child should be completely protected from the dangers of this world, including mental dangers for which he or she is not emotionally ready. My father was in a psychiatric hospital for years. We only visited him that one time, but the impression and odors have never left me. Watching horror movies at the drive-in at age five made such an impression that they gave me nightmares for years afterward.

Understanding, Love, and Forgiveness

Home is where a child is known and learns to know, forgive, and love others—even when they're not perfect. When a parent apologizes or forgives a child, it teaches valuable life lessons. When I look back at all the times my aunt or uncle intervened, it is obvious to me that they knew me. They knew my weaknesses and were observant enough to know when I was doing something I shouldn't be doing. What if they hadn't spoken to me about my relationship with David? Would I, too, be serving time in prison?

Tradition

Home is the place a child remembers when faced with hardship. Create fond memories of time together by instituting daily, weekly, monthly, and annual family traditions. Traditions provide a sense of security because they are predictable. Nothing imprints family memories like family vacations away from the hustle and bustle of everyday life. Memories give us comforting scenes from childhood to return to again and again. And when those comforting customs include spiritual traditions, the "home" a child will return to is a place of faith. Typically, American parents emphasize achievement in school, sports, and wealth over spiritual and sacrificial growth. I wonder what would happen if parents began rewarding children for showing kindness, giving up their "rights," and resolving conflict?

LESSON 2

Children Need Responsibilities

The dust, the grime, the boiling sun, the sleeting rain, the bitter cold, the sweat of the brow: these are the adventures of a Kansas boy hard at work on the farm. There wasn't much I didn't do on the farm. From the cleaning of dusty grain bins to raking manure, I became a seasoned farmhand. I shoveled, raked, cleaned, picked, weeded, planted, fertilized, scraped, dug, climbed, ran, jumped, and killed animals so we would have food on the table. I eventually learned to drive the tractor, an exciting feat for a teenage boy. Looking back, I can see that my work ethic was formed on the farm.

Every child can benefit from responsibilities, or chores, that contribute to the livelihood of the family. Through these they learn the value of hard work and the rewards that a job well done can bring: pride and a sense of accomplishment and appreciating the value of a dollar.

Most people have heard the saying "running around like a chicken with its head cut off." Until you've experienced it up close and personal, you can only imagine what it really means. The gist of the work is that you stretch the chicken's neck across a stump of wood and lower the axe. The chicken is then released, and that's when the action starts.

In spite of the fact that the head is no longer attached to the body, the tiny chicken synapses that fired frantic signals to the chicken's legs are still in transit. When received by the legs, of course, the chicken runs and jumps around for a few seconds, and…well you get the picture.

Here's the point: the person with purpose is not a victim running around like a chicken after the slaughter. Learning to work hard and becoming a man were priceless lessons for a young boy who needed a sense of direction. Before moving to the farm, I was scared and unsure of myself. I needed guidance and a sense of responsibility. I needed to assume ownership of my destiny. My chores gave me a sense that I could impact my own future.

Knowing that you earn your food, shelter, and clothing teaches an appreciation for what you hold in your hands. I was especially lucky to see how my daily bread was tied to the land and life around me. In my youth, I delivered newspapers, cleaned toilets, waxed floors, detasseled corn, weeded our garden, worked at a bowling alley, and threw thousands of bales of hay each summer for a chance to earn my keep and my own financial freedom.

My aunt and uncle also taught me how to budget my time and money, including tithing to my local church and giving to missions. I cleaned my own room; did my own laundry; and bought my own toothpaste, shampoo, and underwear. I learned order and organization and the value of working hard to achieve a goal. This work ethic prepared me for life in a variety of ways and has stood the test of time as life continues to unfold.

I also enjoyed times of play as I grew up. Vacations, ball games, and other fun things, however, were earned rather than simply handed to me. My sense of purpose came from hard work and earning my way. Today I still work from a monthly budget and organize my day and my belongings.

Life-management lessons are essential for today's children. It's natural for parents to want to provide more for their kids than they had, but those desires must be tempered by the reality that most things in life are not free.

While sometimes difficult to grasp and much harder to teach, life-management skills—such as focus, goal orientation, working hard, and organizing to complete tasks—move children down the road toward maturity, professional success, and personal satisfaction.

The sense of pride and dignity we get from doing a job well is the lesson; the monetary reward is secondary. Those are lessons worth learning for any child.

LESSON 3

Kids Need Friends Who Are Headed in the Right Direction

All of us need friends, but we need friends who are going in the right direction. That's a lesson all teenagers must learn. But there's a lesson here for parents too: we cannot choose our children's friends. We think we can, but in reality, we simply can't select their friends for them once they get to a certain age.

What we can do is influence them, as my aunt and uncle did concerning my association with David. At some point, each child has to learn how to choose friends and set his or her own moral direction. Wise parents—as my aunt and uncle seemed to know instinctively—don't exasperate their children—especially when they're teenagers. The apostle Paul tells us, "Don't exasperate your children by coming down hard on them. Take them by the hand and lead them in the way of the Master" (Ephesians 6:4 MSG). Wise parents find ways to help teens see the path before them and where each decision may lead.

In a very real way, teenagers feel the push and pull described by Paul in Romans 7, but for them the temptation is manifested in their friendships. They feel it every moment of every day. They are tempted to swear, drink alcohol, have sex, lie to their parents and teachers, sneak out at night, watch explicit movies, or simply defy authority. It's in their nature. How parents respond can make all the difference. The key is influencing their friendships rather than trying to control.

LESSON 4

Parents Need to Come to Terms with Their Past

Learning our own life lessons is foundational to parenting. Whether abandoned, indulged, ignored, or spoiled as children ourselves, we must learn from the hand we were dealt. Each of us must deal with our past and its influences on our parenting, our family systems, our conflict styles, and our values. We can't teach our children lessons we have not learned ourselves. How we respond to our past will become a blueprint for their future.

So often the past reaches out to grab us. Wanting to hurt us yet again, it crushes us in its grip, leaving us breathless and gasping for air. We desperately want to escape but don't know how. The past is like a vehicle careening down the road, aimed at our children. Unless we are alert, our children will suffer the consequences for our past. We will continue the unhealthy cycle.

The flood of our past feelings comes in various forms: a word, an action, an event, or a thought. In that brief moment, the waves of the past wash over us, leaving us wondering what happened. The real pain manifests itself when we let the past maul our present. It most directly shows itself in our relationships. When past feelings and experiences alienate us from others, we have allowed the pain of the past to rule us.

How we can be hurt time and time again by things in our past is a mystery that defies human comprehension. Just when I thought I had conquered the hurt and pain—when I was confident that the past would never raise its ugly head again—there, in vivid color, is the pain of days gone by. For me, the pain of abandonment reared its ugly head in my relationships with my wife and children. I don't want them to feel abandoned, so I hold on tight and struggle to let them fail and learn their own painful but important lessons.

Many times those closest to us have no knowledge of the feelings we are experiencing. But when we talk with them about our past, our feelings, and our triggers, we set the stage for growth and find hope for the future. Mature, healthy adults know to seek help when the past is controlling them. Whatever your pain—and we all carry childhood pain—find a way to come to terms with it so it doesn't control you—so you don't pass the cycle on to another generation.

No one can forget the past, but you can keep making strides toward recovery as you release your pain and anger. Choosing to move toward understanding, forgiveness, and acceptance of what is past and cannot be changed moves us closer to lasting hope and peace. We cannot change our history, but we can change our future.

LESSON 5

Build Character through Discipline

Discipline is like building fences with gates that are opened or locked in all the right places at the right times. If a child climbs over or crawls under the fence, he experiences natural and logical consequences. When appropriate boundaries become internalized, a child learns self-control and how to make his own moral decisions. He becomes a man of "character" or "integrity." He has a strong internal sense of right and wrong because the fences are solid. He has self-control and can say no to things that are harmful to him or to others.

Discipline should not be confused with punishment. Punishment leads to fear. Appropriate discipline gives a sense of security. The goal of punishment is to inflict enough pain to prevent a child from repeating a wrong or dangerous act. The goal of discipline is to teach a child; it's doesn't have to be painful. Punishment forces constraints on children. Discipline teaches boundaries that children can embrace. Punishment focuses on external behavior. Discipline focuses on the heart. Punishment limits a child. Discipline liberates a child to reach his or her potential.

Boundaries help children know what is appropriate or inappropriate in any given situation. Over time, they learn to adapt and apply the rules to other circumstances. Boundaries are the seeds of respect for others and respect for self. Failure to set boundaries for children nearly always guarantees that they will struggle at work, in school, and in relationships. Life will be more difficult when they grow up.

On the farm, three things defined my boundaries:

1. *Clearly stated and enforced rules.* When I broke the rules, the discipline was consistent. If I was disrespectful, I received a spanking. If I failed to do a chore, I was given an extra chore. If I broke a rule, I had to do something related to that rule. Because they were consistent with me, as I got older, my aunt and uncle were able to influence me in other ways when I stepped outside their boundaries.

2. *Parental figures who did not exasperate me even though I was a troubled and angry young man.* Once, my aunt found a pornographic magazine in my room. Instead of confronting me with it, she laid it on my bed next to my Bible with a short note: "You choose. Choose wisely." I threw that magazine away and never picked one up again. What if she had yelled and screamed at me, lectured me, or shamed me? I wonder if I would have tossed the magazine away and whether my relationship with my wife would be what it is today.

3. *A community that supported my aunt and uncle's efforts to teach me right from wrong.* Parents cannot raise children alone. My aunt and uncle's church friends and the community kept them apprised of my activities. There was very little I was able to keep hidden from their watchful eyes. And for a troubled young man such as me, that was a good thing.

LESSON 6

Show Children Where to Find Wisdom beyond Their Years

Decision-making is dauntingly difficult for many of us. Should we move to that new town for a new job? Should we buy a new car or try to keep the old one running for another year?

Children need a light to guide them, something outside themselves to turn to when they don't have the answers. This external source of right and wrong is you, other adults, good books, and the Bible. The greatest reservoir of wise and not-so-wise decisions by mere mortals is contained within the pages of the Bible. Teach your children to turn to the Bible for guidance at a young age. Over time, they will internalize those values.

Practice what you preach, and apply biblical principles to your own life. Talk about a wrong choice you made as a young person and how admitting that you were wrong made a difference in your life. That's how children learn to make right choices. Applying knowledge to life in such a way as to benefit oneself, others, and God is wisdom.

Never do something for your children that they can do for themselves—including solving their problems, soothing over relationship conflicts, or helping them avoid the consequences of their poor choices.

It takes courage to make a wise decision. Every parent wants his or her children to be strong, to endure difficulties, and overcome obstacles that can hinder them from reaching their goals.

True courage is birthed in adversity. It grows with each challenge we face. When children work through a problem, by making wise decisions and exhibiting courage to do the right thing, they become wise beyond their years.

LESSON 7

Be a Dream Builder, Not a Dream Killer

In order to thrive after they leave their childhood home, kids need their guardians and appointed caregivers to believe in and help build their dreams. Obsession is never a good thing, but being driven within controlled parameters can be a component of success. When nurtured, dreams push us to work hard and make the sacrifices necessary in life. You have two choices when your child says, "I'm going to be the first woman president of the United States": You can say, "Well, then, you're going to have to get better grades." Or you can say, "You can do anything you set your mind to, honey.

You're an extremely smart person." The former are the words of dream killers. The latter are the words of dream builders. They have faith in their children. Which one are you?

To be dream builders, parents need to instill in their children both courage and optimism. Allow them to experience success and failure in small things while very young. As they grow, they will gain courage to make bigger decisions that are open before them. When parents solve problems for children or overprotect them, they steal their opportunity to learn, to endure, and to overcome. They rob their children of a chance to grow in confidence.

To thrive and dream, every child needs healthy doses of old-fashioned faith and optimism. When obstacles get in the way of achieving our goals, encouragement, prayer, and optimism help all of us push onward. Model for your children how to live every day with openness, anticipation, and trust in God. Kids watch how the adults in their lives handle problems, failures, and successes. They do as we do, not as we say.

If we depend on God when things go awry, if we learn from mistakes, if we rejoice in others' successes, our children will follow our example. When bad things happen, we can remind our children that God is in control and with us in every situation. He's our source of confidence when we lack the courage to face something or someone on our own.

When parents show courage and optimism, children are more likely to dream big and to be less afraid to pursue dreams.

LESSON 8

Give Kids Less Showtime and More Playtime

Children need the freedom to be what God created them to be: children. They need to be amazed at new discoveries. They need to feel the pride and joy of completing their science project. They need the liberty to laugh at silly things, to wiggle in their chairs, and to have fun. They also need their parents to be silly, be proud, and wiggle with them on a regular basis. Children need to play!

The imaginations of children today are too often limited by the comforts of life and the ease of fun. Our "grab the gusto now" society, dependence on technology for fun, and the speeding-bullet pace of life can rob children of the time needed to look beyond the here and now. It snatches away the moments of wonderment God intends for them as they grow. The end result is kids who don't know how to use their imagination to dream dreams for the future.

Role-playing and pretending are the stuff from which dreams and goals are formed. Try turning off the TV and video games and challenging your child to exercise his or her brain. Give preschool children empty boxes, sheets, and dress-up clothing instead of technological toys. Role-playing is what helps kids imagine what it might be like to someday have a career.

Kids are heard to exclaim on a daily basis, "I'm bored." Instead of rushing to find the latest movie or video game, encourage them to stretch their imagination and dream dreams.

Conclusion

As a parent, you can give your children what is needed to thrive in spirit and soul. You can give them the strength, wisdom, and character needed to prevent cockleburs from adhering to their spirits and hampering their maturity. This kind of parenting requires diligence, honesty, and faith.

We're not perfect, but that's the curse, and the joy, of parenting. The parent-child relationship is the one relationship that will most expose our weaknesses. On the flip side, it sheds light on our own humanity as we work on becoming better people—hopefully with the help of God, loving friends, and a church community.

Maybe right now you're saying, "It's too late, I've already failed in so many ways." Every parent has failed in many ways. You are not alone. It is better to start now to be a more involved, more loving, more concerned parent than to have never cared or tried. Perfect families are an illusion. All families have flaws. Some are just more transparent about their struggles.

Former all-star pitcher Tim Burke said in his book, *Major League Dad*, "Baseball is going to do just fine without me; it's not going to miss a beat. But I'm the only father my children have. I'm the only husband my wife has. And they need me a lot more than baseball does." That's why he stepped away from the sport at a relatively young age.

That principle holds true for each of us. You're the only father or mother your kids know. You are the most important role model they will ever observe. If something is preventing you from being that role model, change it. Adjust your priorities, how you spend your time, and what you spend your money on in order to become the parent you truly want to be.

It takes strength and wisdom to undertake the greatest task ever given to men and women, to be the father or mother your child needs and deserves. You have to be willing to acknowledge your weaknesses. You have to do the hard work of growing and maturing. You may have to sacrifice doing some of the things you'd like to do. You have to be responsible, understanding, and patient.

But believe me, it's worth it. In the end, you'll be a better person, you'll have a better relationship with your children, and you'll know you did your best. Most importantly, when you get to heaven and see your children there, nothing on earth will matter—not climbing the corporate ladder, not earning more money, not being able to party with your friends—none of it.

Take it from me, a soul survivor saved by faith and love, there is nothing more significant in life.

It's one day, one lesson, one child, at a time. The fate of humanity depends on it.